617.6 THO

Thomas, Pat, 1959-
Do I have to go to the
dentist? : a first look at

First edition for the United States and Canada published
in 2008 by Barron's Educational Series, Inc.

First edition of *Do I Have to Go to the Dentist?*
first published for Great Britain in 2008 by Wayland,
a division of Hachette Children's Books

*All inquiries should be addressed to:*
Barron's Educational Series, Inc.
250 Wireless Boulevard
Hauppauge, New York 11788
*www.barronseduc.com*

Library of Congress Control Number: 2008926685

ISBN-13: 978-0-7641-3901-7
ISBN-10: 0-7641-3901-0

Printed in China
9 8 7 6 5 4 3 2 1

# Do I Have to Go to the Dentist?

A FIRST LOOK AT HEALTHY TEETH

PAT THOMAS
ILLUSTRATED BY LESLEY HARKER

BARRON'S

Before you brush your teeth tonight, think about all the things you couldn't do if they weren't there.

Without your teeth you couldn't
sing or smile or speak clearly,
or bite into a crunchy apple.
You couldn't make funny faces.
It would be hard to pretend
to be a snarling dog or
a roaring lion.

That's why it's important to look after your teeth. And most of the time it's easy to take care of them yourself.

You can do this by not eating sweet or sticky snacks and drinks. Also make sure you brush your teeth really well after meals and before you go to bed.

But sometimes it's good to
have a little extra help
with taking care of
ourselves.

The person who helps us take care of our teeth
is a special kind of doctor called a dentist.

## What about you?

Can you think of other people who help us take care of ourselves?

How do they help us?

Why do you think we need their help?

If you have never been to the dentist,
you may wonder what it will be like.

Some of your friends
or family may have
teased you or told
you scary stories about
going to the dentist.
This might make
you feel worried.

But no one should feel
worried about going
to the dentist.

Your dentist is there to help take care of you.
Your parents or caregivers trust him or her
and you can, too.

## What about you?

What do you know about dentists?
Do you know people who have gone to a dentist?
What have they told you?

Most dentists' offices are busy. Sometimes you have to wait before you can be seen. But usually there are toys to play with and books to read.

When it's your turn, you'll be taken
into a room with a big chair that
goes up and down. There will also
be equipment like special brushes
and a big bright light to help
the dentist see inside
your mouth.

You'll wear a big bib that keeps your clothes clean. Even grown-ups wear this.

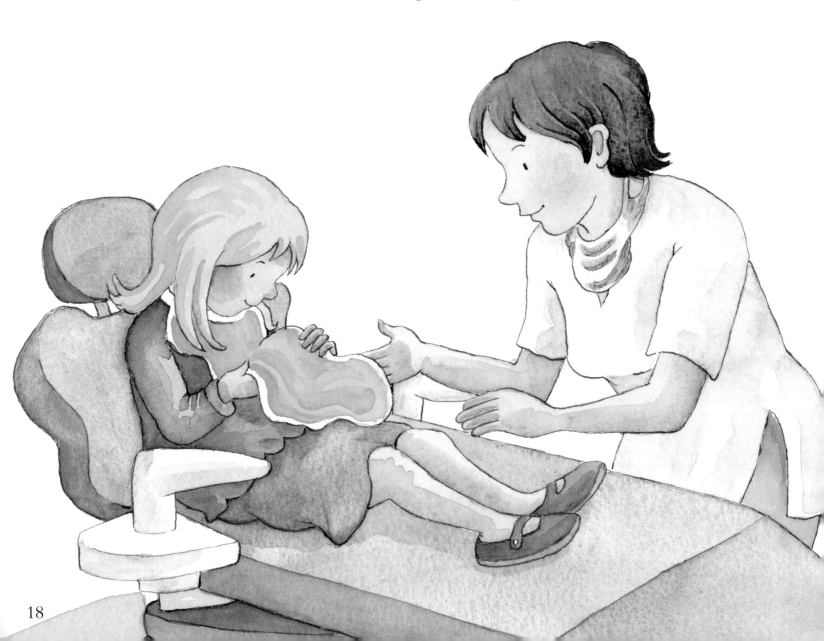

Your dentist will check that your teeth are clean and that new teeth are growing in straight. A check will also be made for any cavities, or holes, in your teeth.

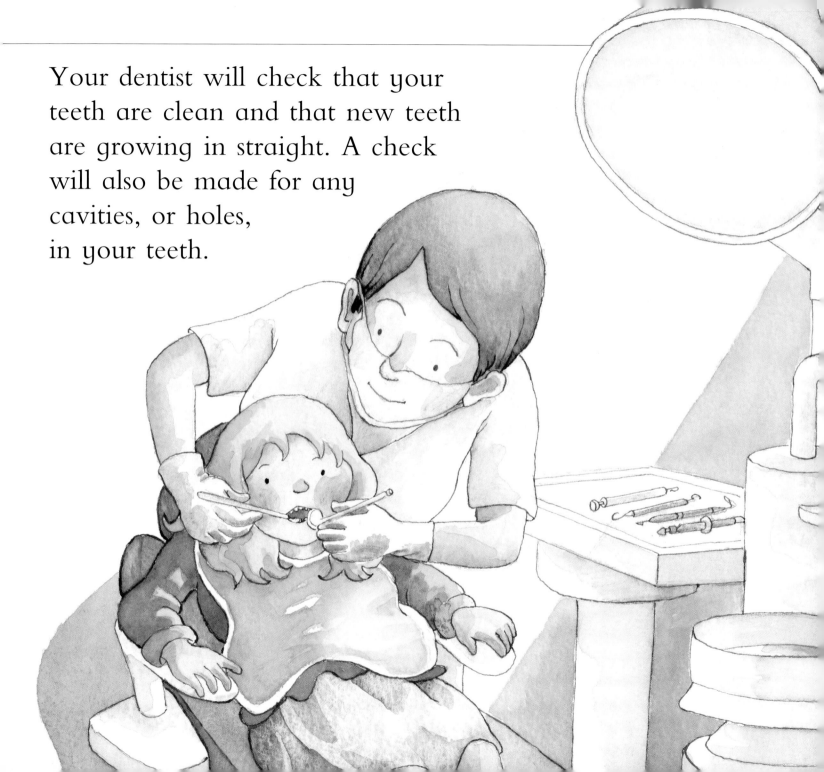

At every visit your dentist will also give
your teeth a really good cleaning with an
electric brush and polishing paste.

It's a bit noisy and it tickles a little as it whizzes around your mouth, but it leaves your teeth smooth and shiny.

A cavity is caused by germs and bits of food
left on your teeth if you don't brush properly.

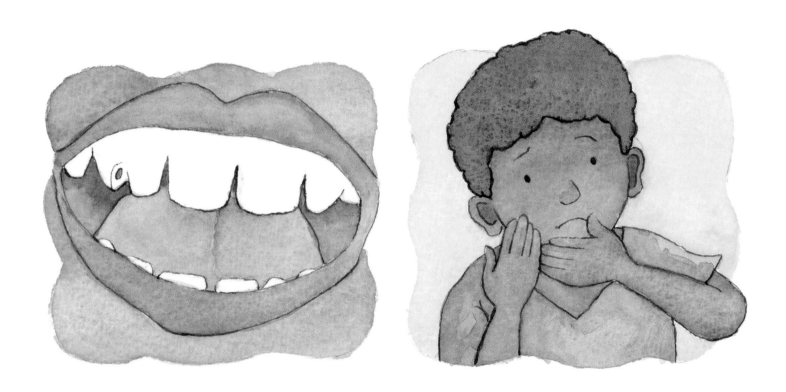

The cavity can get bigger and deeper and
become painful if it isn't fixed.

Sometimes the dentist will take pictures of your teeth to see if you have any cavities that may be hiding in places that can't easily be seen or to check the size of a cavity.

If you have a cavity, the dentist might put your tooth to sleep while a special mixture, called a filling, is prepared.

Before the visit is over, the dentist will
talk to you about the best ways
to care for your teeth.

Your teeth aren't just for smiling—or snarling. They also help you chew so you get all the goodness out of your food. So when your teeth are healthy, the rest of you is, too.

And that's a very good
reason to smile.

# HOW TO USE THIS BOOK

Going to the dentist is one of life's necessities. It may not always be fun, but neither does it have to be traumatic.

The best way to help your child appreciate the importance of going to the dentist is to get him or her used to it from an early age. Current recommendations are that the child's first dental visit be six months after the first tooth has erupted or by age one. Early check-ups are usually quick and easy and help your child get used to what a dentist's office looks, sounds, and smells like. They also ensure that your child gets into the routine of having his or her teeth checked regularly, which helps to identify and minimize tooth problems.

Most children who are anxious about visiting the dentist pick up their parents' dental anxieties; wherever possible, lead by example. Even before your child is ready to go to the dentist, you can take him or her along on one of your own visits. With some children it may help if there is another adult with you to look after your child while you're having a check-up. This allows your child to observe what's going on. Even if you are not totally comfortable at the dentist, it is important to put on a calm, relaxed face—one that portrays a dental check-up as a normal part of life.

In the same vein, don't let your friends or the child's siblings scare your child with stories about their own "bad" experiences with a dentist. Watch your language when your child is at the dentist; avoid using words like "hurt" or "pain" or "brave."

Despite the myths and scare stories that children may hear from friends and family, most dentists are friendly, competent, and not at all scary. It is important, however, that your dentist is skilled at working with children and understands your child's needs (for instance, if your child wishes to have you there during examinations). If you or your child is not happy with a particular dentist—even one you have been going to for years—find another one that suits your child better.

Never use a visit to the dentist as a threat to get your child to avoid sweets or take care of his or her teeth. Instead, set a good example by eating well yourself and, ideally, brushing your own teeth after meals and before bed. With very young children, always supervise brushing to make sure it is done properly.

Play dentist with your children. Check teddy's teeth for cavities (use a toy camera to take an x-ray); teach dolls (or stuffed animals) to brush properly. All these things will help your child learn to take care of his or her teeth and become familiar with the kinds of procedures he or she may be exposed to in a dentist's office.

The importance of caring for teeth and gums is part of every school health curriculum from a very early age. Schools can help familiarize children with the dentist by arranging visits from practitioners in the local community. They can talk to children about the importance of good oral health and how dentists contribute to it. Such visits can certainly help children cope better when they do have to go to the dentist.

# BOOKS TO READ

**Just Going to the Dentist**
Mercer Mayer (Random House, 2001)

**The Berenstain Bears Visit the Dentist**
Stan and Jan Berenstain (Random House, 1981)

**Going to the Dentist** (Pebble Books)
Helen Frost (Capstone Press, 1999)

**What to Expect When You Go to the Dentist**
Heidi Murkoff (HarperFestival, 2002)

FOR PARENTS
**Nothin' Personal Doc, But I Hate Dentists!**
McHenry Lee, Joleen Jackson, and Vicki J. Audette
(IHD Publishing, 1999)

# RESOURCES

**American Academy of Pediatric Dentistry**
211 East Chicago Avenue, Suite 1700
Chicago, Illinois 60611-2663
Tel: (312) 337-2169
Fax: (312) 337-6329
Web: www.aapd.org/pediatricinformation/faq.asp

**American Academy of Pediatrics**
The American Academy of Pediatrics
141 Northwest Point Boulevard
Elk Grove Village, Illinois 60007-1098
Tel: (847) 434-4000
Fax: (847) 434-8000
Web: http://www.aap.org/healthtopics/oralhealth.cfm

**The American Dental Hygienists Association**
http://www.adha.org/oralhealth/children.htm

**National Institute of Dental and Craniofacial Research**
National Institutes of Health
Bethesda, Maryland 20892-2190
Tel: (301) 496-4261
e-mail: nidcrinfo@mail.nih.gov
Web: www.nider.nih.gov

**Canadian Academy of Pediatric Dentistry**
http://www.capd-acdp.org

**The Canadian Dental Hygienists Association**
http://www.cdha.ca
www.smilecity.ca

**Keep Kids Healthy.com**
http://www.keepkidshealthy.com/WELCOME/
    treatmentguides/dental_health.html